resti

Sometimes we need to reclaim and introduce resting boss face. Resting boss face, also known as RBF, is a facial expression of a woman in charge. She may unintentionally appear powerful, authoritative, and confident. This is because she is a boss and her resting state reflects her leadership prowess. The next time someone asks you to smile, feel free to rock the RBF instead – we have work to do, after all.

About nu rule

nu rule notebooks are ruled notebooks made for womxn and our allies. Nu is the pronunciation of "女", the Chinese word for woman. nu rule represents the modern movement for female empowerment. By leading in offices, classrooms, governments, and beyond, we are establishing a new rule.

A portion of the proceeds from every notebook is donated to nonprofits devoted to elevating womxn. Thank you for supporting us as we lift each other up to succeed together.